O9-BTL-024

Women for

A LOVE SO REAL

Readings and Scripture
for the Heart of a Woman

for Women

A
Love So
Real

Readings and Scripture
for the Heart of a Woman

A LOVE SO REAL:

Readings and Scriptures for the Heart of a Woman

Printed in the United States of America
ISBN 0-8054-3148-9

To order additional copies of this book,
call 1-800-448-8032.

1 2 3 4 07 06 05 04

CONTENTS

INTRODUCTION

This is not the kind of book you'll read from cover to cover, most likely. If you do, you may miss much of the impact God's Word can have on your heart.

Instead, this is one of those books that will hopefully find itself in various locations throughout your house—atop your Bible, upside down on a bedside table, near the phone book and the sticky notes around your desk or kitchen counter.

If it is, then you'll be able to best enjoy these quick doses of refreshment and renewal—to meet with God in the middle of an average day and return to the action with your heart enlivened.

That's because this is a book that helps you be honest about where you are, yet ultimately confident in who God is making of you.

So come celebrate the Lord anytime you feel the need. This book, filled with the promises of Scripture and the love of God—so real—will always be here for you . . . in whatever place and whatever condition you find it.

*S*implicity

*D*on't worry
about anything,
but in everything,
through prayer and
petition with thanksgiving,
let your requests be made
known to God.
And the peace of God,
which surpasses
every thought,
will guard your hearts
and your minds
in Christ Jesus.

Philippians 4:6–7

The Simpler Life?

*W*hat would simplicity look like if it showed up on your doorstep in the morning?

Would it filter through your purse, removing all the crinkly candy wrappers, every dried-up ballpoint, the cash receipt for bread, milk, and whatever else you picked up on the twelfth of last month for $5.53 plus tax?

Would it start crossing off whole afternoons of errands from your pocket calendar, freeing up your Friday nights, paying for a few meals out each week, and coming up with a schedule you could pull off without breathing hard?

Would it show you which crate next year's winter clothes are hidden in before your kids are two winters too big for them?

Would it take ten years' worth of photos out of the big shoeboxes in the back closet and arrange them by theme and other natural groupings in fancy, stickered scrapbooks?

Would it type up and catalog your favorite recipes on the computer, update your Christmas card addresses, and balance your last three bank statements before you even went to bed tonight?

Wouldn't that be nice?

But if you're counting on simplicity coming in on the afternoon bus, you're probably in for a long wait. It never makes anything similar to a surprise appearance, and rarely sneaks in unnoticed while you're out driving your children to Scouts and soccer or hustling ten minutes late to a three o'clock meeting.

Simplicity doesn't just happen.

Simplicity has to be sought.

Sometimes it's found by saying "no"—by realizing that a night at home isn't always a concession to selfishness but a much-needed time to be still, to slow down. Sometimes it's found by saying "yes"—by making the brave decision to take control of the things in your schedule that are robbing from you the peace of doing less, thanks to the option of doing everything.

More times than not, though, simplicity must be found between the bulges on your lengthy list of things to do. Even on days when life seems bigger than your best efforts, there is simplicity to be found if you look for it.

God gives us simplicity, for example, in the pastel yellow wings of a butterfly, flitting lazily just outside your windshield at a crowded intersection. He gives simplicity in the soft skin of a one-year-old, fresh from the bath and still smelling of shampoo and baby lotion.

He gives simplicity in the soothing aroma of good coffee, in the crisp feel of fresh sheets and pillowcases, in the regular reminder to pray for the people whose pictures are plastered on your refrigerator.

At times God helps us succeed in bringing order into our lives, and sweet simplicity follows. Yet when order has disintegrated into near chaos, he can show us—if we'll let him—how to rescue simplicity from the jaws of runaway activity.

Simplicity is his promise . . . a peace he reserves not only for those who appear to have it all together, but also for those of us who just seem to have it all to do.

Peace I leave with you. My peace I give to you. I do not give to you as the world gives. Your heart must not be troubled or fearful.

John 14:27

The Spirit Himself testifies together with our spirit that we are God's children, and if children, also heirs—heirs of God and co-heirs with Christ—seeing that we suffer with Him so that we may also be glorified with Him.

For I consider that the sufferings of this present time are not worth comparing with the glory that is going to be revealed to us.

Romans 8:16–18

This is why I tell you: Don't worry about your life, what you will eat or what you will drink; or about your body, what you will wear. Isn't life more than food and the body more than clothing? Look at the birds of the sky: they don't sow or reap or gather into barns, yet your heavenly Father feeds them. Aren't you worth more than they?

Matthew 6:25–26

No one can be a slave of two masters, since either he will hate one and love the other, or be devoted to one and despise the other. You cannot be slaves of God and of money.

Matthew 6:24

And why do you worry about clothes? Learn how the wildflowers of the field grow: they don't labor or spin thread. Yet I tell you that not even Solomon in all his splendor was adorned like one of these!

If that's how God clothes the grass of the field, which is here today and thrown into the furnace tomorrow, won't He do much more for you—you of little faith?

Matthew 6:28–30

Come to Me, all you who are weary and burdened, and I will give you rest. Take My yoke upon you and learn from Me, because I am gentle and humble in heart, and you will find rest for your souls.

Matthew 11:28–29

One day [Jesus] and His disciples got into a boat. . . . They set out, and as they were sailing He fell asleep. Then a fierce windstorm came down on the lake; they were being swamped and were in danger. They came and woke Him up, saying, "Master, Master, we're going to die!" Then He got up and rebuked the wind and the raging waves. So they ceased, and there was a calm. He said to them, "Where is your faith?" They were fearful and amazed, saying to one another, "Who can this be? He commands even the winds and the waves, and they obey Him!"

Luke 8:22–25

The Bible gives me a deep, comforting
sense that things seen are temporal,
and things unseen are eternal.

–Helen Keller

$\mathcal{N}$ow the end of all things is near; therefore, be clear-headed and disciplined for prayer.

Above all, keep your love for one another at full strength, since love covers a multitude of sins. Be hospitable to one another without complaining.

Based on the gift they have received, everyone should use it to serve others, as good managers of the varied grace of God.

If anyone speaks, his speech should be like the oracles of God; if anyone serves, his service should be from the strength God provides, so that in everything God may be glorified through Jesus Christ. To Him belong the glory and the power forever and ever. Amen.

1 Peter 4:7–11

A Sabbath rest remains, therefore, for God's people. For the person who has entered His rest has rested from his own works, just as God did from His.

Hebrews 4:9–10

I am the bread of life," Jesus told them. "No one who comes to Me will ever be hungry, and no one who believes in Me will ever be thirsty again."

John 6:35

Then Jesus spoke to them again: "I am the light of the world. Anyone who follows Me will never walk in the darkness, but will have the light of life."

John 8:12

Though I am afflicted and needy,
the LORD thinks of me.
You are my help and my deliverer;
my God, do not delay.

Psalm 40:17

Quiet

The result of righteousness will be peace; the effect of righteousness will be quiet confidence forever. Then My people will dwell in a peaceful place, and in safe and restful dwellings.

Isaiah 32:17–18

Let There Be Quiet

*I*s there a quiet place in your day?

Maybe it's before sunrise—the windows still dark, the air still a bit chilly except for the warmth of a crocheted blanket thrown over your lap. The day is fresh and ahead of you, unspoiled, untouched. Your Bible lies open, your prayers are thoughts and whispers. Just you. And God.

Maybe it's sometime in the early afternoon. The kids are napping. The traffic still sails by outside where you could hear it if you wanted to. But you don't. You're alone for a few stolen moments . . . enjoying a snack, enjoying a book, enjoying a minute to yourself.

Maybe it's late at night. The clock that ticked unnoticeably all evening is now regular and audible, your PJs on, your TV off.

You sink into the couch pillows, almost dozing but not ready for bed yet, almost able to put your worries out of your mind, almost too comfortable for words.

Maybe your quiet time is some other time.

Or maybe it's never.

But it's never too late to make time for it.

Over and over in Jesus' life, you see this one who was so busy, who was caught up in so many stressful situations, who was tugged on and clawed at from so many different people . . . getting away, stealing off, seeking quiet.

Sometimes it was night—even all night. Sometimes it was early in the morning, long before his friends and disciples had stirred from sleep. At the end of a long day or before the start of a new one, he yearned for quiet, for time spent alone with his heavenly Father, for the secret hours his human side needed in order to sort out what was going on in his life.

And if Jesus himself needed quiet, certainly we all need quiet.

But quiet won't come looking for you. You'll have to wrestle it away from a world grown noisy and demanding, from a culture that rushes to fill every second with sound and movement and high-speed information. You'll have to plan for it, draw boundary lines around it, protect it from phone calls and talk shows and even your own impatience. You'll be tempted to think you can live without it, but you'll only end up joining the rest of us who have had to learn the hard way— through four-day flu bugs and weekend fatigue— that if we don't take responsibility for slowing ourselves down, our bodies will do it for us.

The simple truth is that quiet time spent with the Lord, with his Word and our own hearts laid open before him, will never take more away from us than it gives back to us. It will always replenish, always add to the life of our days, and most likely even add to the days of our lives.

Enjoy the blessings of being quiet.

$\mathcal{I}$ said, "If only I had wings like a dove!
  I would fly away and find rest.
How far away I would flee;
  I would stay in the wilderness.
I would hurry to my shelter
  from the raging wind and the storm."

Psalm 55:6–8

$\mathcal{T}$his is what the Lord says,
  "Stand by the roadways and look.
Ask about the ancient paths,
  where the good way is,
    then walk on it and find rest for yourselves."

Jeremiah 6:16a

$\mathcal{T}$he Lord God, the Holy One of Israel,
has said: "You will be delivered by returning
and resting; your strength will lie in quiet
confidence."

Isaiah 30:15a

$\mathcal{C}$almness puts great sins to rest.

Ecclesiastes 10:4b

When I observe Your heavens,
  the work of Your fingers,
  the moon and the stars,
  which You set in place,
  what is man, that You remember him,
  the son of man, that You look after him?
You made him little less than God
  and crowned him with glory and honor.

Psalm 8:3–5

The LORD is good
  to those who hope in Him—
  to the one who seeks Him.
It is good for one to wait silently
  for the LORD's salvation.

Lamentations 3:25–26

LORD, my heart is not proud;
  my eyes are not haughty.
I do not get involved with things
  too great or too difficult for me.
Instead, I have calmed and quieted myself
  like a little weaned child with its mother;
  I am like a little child.

Psalm 131:1–2

Trust in the LORD and do good;
  dwell in the land and live securely.
Take delight in the LORD,
  and He will give you your heart's desires.
Commit your way to the LORD;
  trust in Him, and He will act,
  making your righteousness shine like the dawn,
  your justice like the noonday.
Be silent before the LORD
  and wait expectantly for Him.

Psalm 37:3–7a

*The Bible is God's message to every-
body. We deceive ourselves if we claim to
want to hear His voice but neglect the
primary channel through which it comes.*

–Elisabeth Elliot

Sing for joy, Daughter Zion;
  shout loudly, Israel!
Be glad and rejoice with all your heart,
  Daughter Jerusalem!
The LORD has removed your punishment;
  He has turned back your enemy.
The King of Israel, the LORD, is among you;
  you need no longer fear harm.
On that day it will be said to Jerusalem:
  "Do not fear; Zion,
  do not let your hands grow limp.
The LORD your God is among you,
  a warrior who saves.
He rejoices over you with gladness.
  He brings you quietness by His love.
He delights in you with singing."

Zephaniah 3:14–17

On the last and most important day of the festival, Jesus stood up and cried out, "If anyone is thirsty, he should come to Me and drink! The one who believes in Me, as the Scripture has said, will have streams of living water flow from deep within him."

John 7:37–38

Let us go to His dwelling place;
  let us worship at His footstool.
Arise, LORD, come to Your resting place,
  You and the ark that shows Your strength.
May Your priests be clothed with righteousness,
  and may Your godly people shout for joy.

Psalm 132:7–9

Finally brothers, whatever is true, whatever is honorable, whatever is just, whatever is pure, whatever is lovely, whatever is commendable— if there is any moral excellence and if there is any praise—dwell on these things.

Philippians 4:8

Contentment

Though the fig tree does not bud and there is no yield on the vines, though the olive crop fails and the fields produce no food, though there are no sheep in the pen and no cattle in the stalls, yet I will exult in the LORD; I will rejoice in the God of my salvation!

Habakkuk 3:17–18

I'm Okay with That

Of all the blessings that come to us from being a believer in Christ, one of the greatest is this: *an eternal perspective*, the assurance of knowing that God will always remain in full control, that our lives are bigger than the last twenty-four hours.

Good thing, too, because we all know how it feels to be dependent on our circumstances, riding the highs and lows of life, living off the warm bread of compliments and success, only to be buried under the weight of others' unkind remarks or the sudden realization that we have failed at something important to us.

Life can be both bright and brutal.

Yet most of us come into life demanding nothing *but* the bright side, carrying with us a certain set of expectations, ideas about the way things should go for us, the way things should turn out.

Sometimes they do; sometimes they don't.

Then what?

That's when we must cling to something more lasting than a day's turn of events. That's when we must cry out to Someone who has helped countless others through the painful aftermath of a spiritual setback. That's when we must look beyond our dim prospects and see a heavenly future that dims everything in comparison.

This eternal outlook is the secret of our contentment.

It's the fresh sheet of paper laid on a stack of stray scribblings and poor attempts, promising a new start and a hopeful beginning.

It's the gift box that contains an old, ordinary item, worn and scarred by a lifetime of use, now transformed by the years into a valuable heirloom precious enough to bring tears to its receiver's eyes and find itself on proud display in a place of honor.

It's the sturdy foundation of confidence that anchors the floor beneath hospital beds and waiting room chairs, beneath dinner tables shared by one less member of the family, beneath living room rugs where a desperate mother prays for her prodigal.

Because God has promised his people forever, we now have the privilege of enduring today—whatever it brings, whatever it means. Through the full certainty of our tomorrow, we now have the rationale for embracing this afternoon, tucking it inside the will of God, and living it for his glory.

Because the living God has made himself ours, we now have his full permission to lay our situations and circumstances at his feet, and trust that he "has arranged everything appropriately in its time and has also put forever in [our] hearts" (Ecclesiastes 3:11).

And we can be okay with that.

*W*hen I am filled with cares,
   Your comfort brings me joy.

Psalm 94:19

*F*or He crushes, but He also binds up;
He strikes, but His hands also heal.

Job 5:18

*S*o let us know, let us strive to know, the LORD!
   His appearance is as certain as the dawn.
He will come to us like the rain,
   like the spring rain that waters the earth.

Hosea 6:3

I will give praise
   in the great congregation because of You;
I will fulfill my vows
   before those who fear You.
The humble will eat and be satisfied;
   those who seek the LORD will praise Him.

Psalm 22:25–26a

$\mathcal{Y}$our life should be free from the love of money. Be satisfied with what you have, for He Himself has said, I will never leave you or forsake you.

Hebrews 13:5

$\mathcal{J}$f you ever forget the LORD your God and go after other gods, to serve and worship them, I testify against you today that you will surely perish.

Deuteronomy 8:19

$\mathcal{B}$ut godliness with contentment is a great gain. For we brought nothing into the world, and we can take nothing out. But if we have food and clothing, we will be content with these.

But those who want to be rich fall into temptation, a trap, and many foolish and harmful desires, which plunge people into ruin and destruction. For the love of money is a root of all kinds of evil, and by craving it, some have wandered away from the faith and pierced themselves with many pains.

1 Timothy 6:6–10

Two things I ask of You;
   don't deny them to me before I die:
Keep falsehood and deceitful words far from me.
   Give me neither poverty nor wealth;
   feed me with the food I need.
Otherwise, I might have too much
   and deny You, saying, "Who is the LORD?"
   or I might have nothing and steal,
   profaning the name of my God.

Proverbs 30:7–9

The Bible belongs to those elemental
   things — like the sky, the wind, and the
   sea, like the kisses of little children and
   tears shed beside the grave — which can
   never grow stale or out of date.

—T. H. Darlow

$\mathcal{R}$emember this: the person who sows sparingly will also reap sparingly, and the person who sows generously will also reap generously. . . .

And God is able to make every grace overflow to you, so that in every way, always having everything you need, you may excel in every good work. As it is written: "He has scattered; He has given to the poor; His righteousness endures forever."

Now the One who provides seed for the sower and bread for food will provide and multiply your seed and increase the harvest of your righteousness, as you are enriched in every way for all generosity, which produces thanksgiving to God through us.

2 Corinthians 9:6, 8–11

*B*lessed are those who hunger and thirst
for righteousness, because they will be filled.

Matthew 5:6

*H*ow long will I store up
   anxious concerns within me,
   agony in my mind every day? . . .
But I have trusted in Your faithful love;
   my heart will rejoice in Your deliverance.
I will sing to the LORD
   because He has treated me generously.

Psalm 13:2a, 5–6

*D*o not be agitated by evildoers;
   do not envy those who do wrong.
For they wither quickly like grass
   and wilt like tender green plants.

Psalm 37:1–2

*T*he fear of the LORD leads to life;
   one will sleep at night without danger.

Proverbs 19:23

Security

$\mathcal{I}$ keep the LORD in mind always. Because He is at my right hand, I will not be defeated. Therefore my heart is glad, and my spirit rejoices; my body also rests securely.... You reveal the path of life to me; in Your presence is abundant joy; in Your right hand are eternal pleasures.

Psalm 16:8–9, 11

Safe Places

There are young girls who have been born in the past few years—girls who will become grown women living through the balance of this century—who will not remember a time when we could leave paid bills in the mailbox with the flag up and not worry about someone stealing the checks and cashing them for themselves.

They won't know what it's like to take a memory-lane stroll across their old high school campus and not be stopped for questioning by a patrolling security guard. They won't know how it feels to ignore or at best barely notice a plane flying overhead, to not whisper a prayer that its passengers are safe inside.

They won't think back to a day when kids played all over the neighborhood until their mom called them in for dinner, a day before car alarms and metal detectors, a day that came and went without one suspicious stare.

They will have known only a world of purse searches and lockdowns.

Sad, isn't it?

But today we've come to expect these things as the price of our security. We've wisely built tight systems around ourselves to avoid stumbling into danger. We've kept one hand on the mace spray and walked a little faster through the parking lot. But even with the best planning and preparations, we must come to the conclusion that there is no safe place on earth. There never was, really. It just felt that way.

Sure, we may be able to take steps to protect ourselves physically, but there is really no safe place for the human heart, no way to flee from the aging process, no town to move to where people's feelings don't get hurt and where emergency rooms are unnecessary.

We have only one safe place—the same One we've had all along—the same One who put the stars of the Big Dipper, Orion, and the Pleiades in place countless centuries ago (Job 9:9) and still keeps them hanging there in the winter sky. The same One who promised that seedtime and harvest would come around every year (Genesis 8:22) and hasn't missed one since. The same One who prophesied hundreds of years ahead of time that a little virgin girl would have a baby (Isaiah 7:14) and the throne of David would have an everlasting occupant (Isaiah 9:6).

Yes, we do have a safe place, a Father not willing for a hair to slip from our head uncounted (Luke 12:7), a Guardian whose angels are ministering to us in ways we can only imagine (Hebrews 1:14), a Savior willingly injected with the deadly poison of our own sin, who is praying for us right now in heavenly places (Hebrews 7:25).

Some girls may not know a day when the earth was a safe place.

But we should help them know a God who can keep them safe forever.

The LORD is my light and my salvation—
  whom should I fear?
The LORD is the stronghold of my life—
  of whom should I be afraid?

Psalm 27:1

When I am afraid,
  I will trust in You.
In God, whose word I praise,
  in God I trust; I will not fear.
What can man do to me?

Psalm 56:3–4

We have this kind of confidence toward
God through Christ: not that we are competent
in ourselves to consider anything as coming
from ourselves, but our competence is
from God.

2 Corinthians 3:4–5

Therefore if the Son sets you free, you really
will be free.

John 8:36

Your heart must not be troubled. Believe in God; believe also in Me. In My Father's house are many dwelling places; if not, I would have told you. I am going away to prepare a place for you. If I go away and prepare a place for you, I will come back and receive you to Myself, so that where I am you may be also.

John 14:1–3

All who came before Me are thieves and robbers, but the sheep didn't listen to them. I am the door. If anyone enters by Me, he will be saved, and will come in and go out and find pasture. A thief comes only to steal and to kill and to destroy. I have come that they may have life and have it in abundance.

John 10:8–10

I will take you as My wife forever.
I will wed you in righteousness,
    justice, love, and compassion.
I will wed you in faithfulness,
    and you will know the LORD.

Hosea 2:19–20

The LORD is good,
  a stronghold in a day of distress;
He cares for those who take refuge in Him.

Nahum 1:7

He will stand and shepherd them
  in the strength of the LORD,
  in the majestic name of the LORD His God.
They will live securely, for at that time His
  greatness will extend to the ends of the earth.

Micah 5:4

*We need to study the Bible intelligently,
not as if the Scriptures were a sort of
holy rabbit's foot, but for its wisdom in
the broad sweep of its teaching about the
nature of God and of man.*

–Catherine Marshall

*T*he LORD is my shepherd;
    there is nothing I lack.
He lets me lie down in green pastures;
    He leads me beside quiet waters.
He renews my life;
    He leads me along the right paths
    for His name's sake.
Even when I go through the darkest valley,
    I am not afraid of any danger,
    for You are with me;
    Your rod and Your staff—
    they give me comfort.
You prepare a table before me
    in full view of my enemies;
    You anoint my head with oil; my cup is full.
Only goodness and faithful love
    will pursue me all the days of my life,
    and I will dwell in the house of the LORD
    as long as I live.

Psalm 23:1–6

I will leave among you
a meek and humble people,
and they will trust
in the name of the LORD.

Zephaniah 3:12

*T*he name of the LORD is a strong tower;
the righteous run to it and are protected.

Proverbs 18:10

*Y*ou will keep in perfect peace
the mind that is dependent on You,
for it is trusting in You.
Trust in the LORD forever,
because the LORD is an everlasting rock!

Isaiah 26:3–4

*N*ow may the God of hope fill you with
all joy and peace in believing, so that you may
overflow with hope by the power of the Holy
Spirit.

Romans 15:13

Understanding

$\mathscr{I}$ pray that the eyes of your heart may be enlightened so you may know what is the hope of His calling, what are the glorious riches of His inheritance among the saints, and what is the immeasurable greatness of His power to us who believe, according to the working of His vast strength.

Ephesians 1:18–19

I Want to Believe

$\mathcal{M}$any of us have been around church for so long, we never really question whether or not we believe in God. *Of course*, we do. Why else would we be here? But there do come times when we wonder. For example, when we hear of all the different religious beliefs and practices operating in our world, we wonder how there could possibly be just *one way* among all the others held so deeply by so many.

Or when we think of a dear friend who is such a good person but who just can't understand why a relationship with Christ should matter in her life, we wonder if our faith is built on anything more than the way we grew up.

Or when we get into discussions with people who know we're Christians, who ask us those "what do you think about" questions that paint us into a corner and make us sound so prudish and narrow, we wonder if it's just us or our beliefs that have grown tired and dry.

But there's one place where doubts go to die.

And you're no more than a page turn from being there.

The Bible is an anchor of truth in a sea of deception. We can't go to the store, we can't go to the health club, we can't go to work, we can't go down the street without running head-on into deceptive images and ideas. Do this. Be that. Think this. Try that. Go here. Go there. What for? Why not?

It's everywhere. Lies, untruth, deception. Even inside our own homes. Even inside our own hearts.

But it doesn't have to be, because we can open the Word. We can dive in there and swim around in truths that have preserved God's people for generations. We can turn from one book to the next and discover passages and insights we've never even noticed before. We can find it to be as fresh as a question we were asking ourselves just the other day, yet as long-lasting as a verse we remember learning from our childhood.

We can read it. And we can live it.

Some people read their Bible like they're taking a dose a medicine, checking it off their calendar and not thinking about it again till tomorrow. The Scripture says they're like people who look at themselves in a mirror before they leave the house, but when they get out into the real world, they can't remember what they looked like. They live in dread that a hair might be out of place, a lunch stain might have gotten on their clothes, a noticeable flaw might have come unmasked without their knowing it.

But when the Bible is our food and drink, when it's not just words to think about but words to live by, we can march with confidence into our day. We can spot deception for what it is. We can "know whom [we] have believed" (2 Timothy 1:12) and be convinced that his truth will keep us pure and protected in every stage of life.

The question is not whether our minds are open or not. The question is whether our Bibles are.

I have written these things to you who believe in the name of the Son of God, so that you may know that you have eternal life.

1 John 5:13

And we know that the Son of God has come and has given us understanding so that we may know the true One. We are in the true One—that is, in His Son Jesus Christ. He is the true God and eternal life.

1 John 5:20

You love Him, though you have not seen Him. And though not seeing Him now, you believe in Him and rejoice with inexpressible and glorious joy, because you are receiving the goal of your faith, the salvation of your souls.

1 Peter 1:8–9

This is the victory that has conquered the world: our faith. And who is the one who conquers the world but the one who believes that Jesus is the Son of God?

1 John 5:4b–5

*D*ear friends, do not believe every spirit, but test the spirits to determine if they are from God, because many false prophets have gone out into the world.

This is how you know the Spirit of God: Every spirit who confesses that Jesus Christ has come in the flesh is from God. But every spirit who does not confess Jesus is not from God. . . .

You are from God, little children, and you have conquered them, because the One who is in you is greater than the one who is in the world.

1 John 4:1–3a, 4

*T*herefore we will not be afraid,
    though the earth trembles
    and the mountains topple
    into the depths of the seas.

Psalm 46:2

*T*his saying is trustworthy and deserves full acceptance. In fact, we labor and strive for this, because we have put our hope in the living God.

1 Timothy 4:9–10a

Therefore, I will most gladly boast all the more about my weaknesses, so that Christ's power may reside in me. . . . For when I am weak, then I am strong.

2 Corinthians 12:9b, 10b

For our momentary light affliction is producing for us an absolutely incomparable eternal weight of glory. So we do not focus on what is seen, but on what is unseen; for what is seen is temporary, but what is unseen is eternal.

2 Corinthians 4:17–18

It is as silly for a Christian to set out upon the journey of life without the Bible to guide them as it is for a traveler to set off without a map.

–Jill Briscoe

$\mathcal{T}$herefore, brothers, since we have boldness to enter the sanctuary through the blood of Jesus, by the new and living way that He has inaugurated for us, through the curtain (that is, His flesh); and since we have a great high priest over the house of God, let us draw near with a true heart in full assurance of faith, our hearts sprinkled clean from an evil conscience and our bodies washed in pure water.

Let us hold on to the confession of our hope without wavering, for He who promised is faithful. . . . My righteous one will live by faith; and if he draws back, My soul has no pleasure in him. But we are not those who draw back and are destroyed, but those who have faith and obtain life.

Hebrews 10:19–23, 38–39

So don't throw away your confidence, which has a great reward. For you need endurance, so that after you have done God's will, you may receive what was promised.

Hebrews 10:35–37

Before this faith came, we were confined under the law, imprisoned until the coming faith was revealed.

Galatians 3:23

But our citizenship is in heaven, from which we also eagerly wait for a Savior, the Lord Jesus Christ. He will transform the body of our humble condition into the likeness of His glorious body, by the power that enables Him to subject everything to Himself.

Philippians 3:20–21

Now the God of all grace, who called you to His eternal glory in Christ Jesus, will personally restore, establish, strengthen, and support you after you have suffered a little.

1 Peter 5:10

*C*hildren, obey your parents in the Lord, because this is right. Honor your father and mother—which is the first commandment with a promise—that it may go well with you and that you may have a long life in the land.

Ephesians 6:1–3

The Gift of a Child

Not all women are mothers, of course. Some are.

But we have all been children. We have all known what it's like to be three. And seven. And twelve. And fourteen.

For some, these early ages come with memories of dressing up dolls or having friends over for birthday parties. Pretending at tea, working on piano scales, learning to make brownies.

For others, however, these ages aren't the kind of memories we like to think about. We've moved on. We've made it . . . by the hardest. So childhood is something no one can write about in broad brush terms. There are as many women anymore who think of childhood as tragic as there are who think of it as idyllic.

But mothers possess the God-given potential to change all of that.

If you have children, then no matter what being three and seven and twelve and fourteen mean to you, you can make these ages a blessing in the life of your son, your daughter, your children. You can pour God's love into the lives of your kids without guilt or manipulation, and allow them to experience what he can do in a person's heart. You may never be able to fully outrun the harm that was caused you as a child or the pain that you carry as a result, but you can bravely make certain that your child, your children, never have to live under the load you were forced to bear.

You can overcome dullness with life, or if necessary because of your childhood experience, you can overcome evil with good.

But how?

You can teach them the Word. You can make time each day to explore it together. You can wrap your arms around them and pray that God's message always finds a soft place to land in their hearts.

You can talk with them, connecting with them over supper, after school, before bed. You can run through your list of things to do and find several that can wait till later . . . so that you and your children can be together now.

You can help them make good friends. You can help them learn from your experiences. You can help them see the consequences of bad choices . . . and the compound blessings of obedience.

You can encourage them to seek God's will and his best every day. You can connect them with the community of Christian believers, the church. You can model Christlike living in front of them so they'll know it when they see it, so they'll want it when it's their choice to make.

You can also count on this process being a great deal imperfect and wildly time-consuming. But you can persevere. You can stay on your knees. You can keep believing. Even if you're not a parent—or if your parenting years are now behind you—you can love a child that's near you and help them see what God's Word looks like in a big girl's heart.

We often love God best by loving his children.

*T*each a youth about the way he should go;
even when he is old he will not depart from it.

Proverbs 22:6

*L*et Your work be seen by Your servants,
and Your splendor by their children.

Psalm 90:16

*T*ell your children about it,
and let your children tell their children,
and their children the next generation.

Joel 1:3

*W*alk as children of light—for the fruit
of the light results in all goodness, righteousness, and truth—discerning what is pleasing
to the Lord.

Ephesians 5:8b–10

*T*herefore, be imitators of God, as dearly
loved children. And walk in love, as the
Messiah also loved us and gave Himself for
us, a sacrificial and fragrant offering to God.

Ephesians 5:1–2

Come, children, listen to me;
  I will teach you the fear of the LORD.
Who is the man who delights in life,
  loving a long life to enjoy what is good?
Keep your tongue from evil
  and your lips from deceitful speech.
Turn away from evil and do good;
  seek peace and pursue it.

Psalm 34:11–14

In the fear of the LORD one has strong
  confidence and his children have a refuge.

Proverbs 14:26

My little children, I am writing you these
things so that you may not sin. But if anyone
does sin, we have an advocate with the Father—
Jesus Christ the righteous One.

1 John 2:1

For we have become companions of the
Messiah if we hold firmly until the end the
reality that we had at the start.

Hebrews 3:14

*D*on't withhold correction from a youth.

Proverbs 23:13a

*D*iscipline your son,
and he will give you comfort;
he will also give you delight.

Proverbs 29:17

*L*ittle children, we must not love in word
or speech, but in deed and truth.

1 John 3:18

*W*hatever merit there is in anything
that I have written is simply due to the
fact that when I was a child, my mother
daily read me a part of the Bible and
made me learn a part of it by heart.

–John Ruskin

Therefore, get your minds ready for action, being self-disciplined, and set your hope completely on the grace to be brought to you at the revelation of Jesus Christ.

As obedient children, do not be conformed to the desires of your former ignorance but, as the One who called you is holy, you also are to be holy in all your conduct; for it is written, "Be holy, because I am holy."

And if you address as Father the One who judges impartially based on each one's work, you are to conduct yourselves in reverence during this time of temporary residence. . . .

For all flesh is like grass, and all its glory like a flower of the grass. The grass withers, and the flower drops off, but the word of the Lord endures forever. And this is the word that was preached as the gospel to you.

1 Peter 1:13–17, 24–25

See that you don't look down on one of these little ones, because I tell you that in heaven their angels continually view the face of My Father in heaven. . . .

What do you think? If a man has 100 sheep, and one of them goes astray, won't he leave the 99 on the hillside, and go and search for the stray? And if he finds it, I assure you: He rejoices over that sheep more than over the 99 that did not go astray. In the same way, it is not the will of your Father in heaven that one of these little ones perish.

Matthew 18:10, 12–14

Whoever welcomes one little child such as this in My name welcomes Me.

Mark 9:37a

I am not seeking what is yours, but you. For children are not obligated to save up for their parents, but parents for their children. I will most gladly spend and be spent for you.

2 Corinthians 12:14b–15a

Influence

$\mathcal{I}$mpress these words of Mine on your hearts. . . . Teach them to your children, talking about them when you sit in your house and when you walk along the road, when you lie down and when you get up. Write them on the doorposts of your house and on your gates, so that as long as the heavens are above the earth, your days and those of your children may be many.

Deuteronomy 11:18a, 19–21a

Is Anyone Listening?

$\mathscr{M}$any women feel as though they don't have a lot of influence.

You may be a young mother. And while you know that your children depend on you for even their most basic needs, it's still just you and them, in your house, at your street address. It's not like you're making a huge impact on the world or anything. Or so you think.

You may be in middle age. You've done a lot of different things over the course of your life, but when you look back every so often, you ask yourself, "Have I really made any difference?"

You may be, uh, beyond middle age. You may have already raised several children into adulthood. You may be out of the workplace, out of the mainstream, out of circulation. Does anyone care about anything you have to say?

Yes.

You're making an impact.

You're making a difference.

You're making others' lives better.

One of the oddest things going in our current cultural climate is that while we're all becoming more self-sufficient, we're also becoming more aware of our need for others.

With pay-at-the-pump gas stations and self-serve grocery checkouts, we can almost make it through the day without speaking an unnecessary word to a human soul. We can survive pretty much on our own without interacting all that often with the outside world.

But deep inside we know that our calling in life is not simply to accomplish daily tasks as fast as humanly possible or to surround ourselves with comfort and convenience. We know that we need a community. And we know—or we should know—that our community of children, church friends, coworkers, and companions needs us.

They need our encouragement. They need to know that when we promise to be praying for them, it won't be the last time their name enters our minds. They need to know that when we talk with them, they have our full attention, that when we ask how they're doing, we wait for an answer.

They need our counsel. The world is full today of information and opinions. But what your world needs more than any of these are the applied principles of God and the living example of one who has learned to depend on them. Ask God for wisdom. Give it a chance to sink in. And make sure you pass it around.

They need our time. Especially if you still have children under your roof, never forget that you have more opportunities to affect the future through this one, these two, these three—however many—than you do through any other venue of life. Soak them good in God's Word. Saturate them daily in hugs and affection. Surround them at many points throughout the day with prayer and God's presence.

There are many who are listening, who are watching, who are in need.

And they are so glad to have a mom, a sister, a wife, a grandma, a friend like you.

$\mathcal{T}$ake care and diligently watch yourselves, so these things don't slip from your mind all the days of your life. Teach them to your children and your grandchildren.

Deuteronomy 4:9

$\mathcal{A}$nd I pray this: that your love will keep on growing in knowledge and every kind of discernment, so that you can determine what really matters and can be pure and blameless in the day of Christ, filled with the fruit of righteousness that comes through Jesus Christ, to the glory and praise of God.

Philippians 1:9–11

$\mathcal{T}$his is how we know that we love God's children, when we love God and obey His commands. For this is what love for God is: to keep His commands. Now His commands are not a burden, because whatever has been born of God conquers the world.

1 John 5:2–4a

$\mathcal{L}$ove must be without hypocrisy. Detest evil; cling to what is good. Show family affection to one another with brotherly love. Outdo one another in showing honor. Do not lack diligence; be fervent in spirit; serve the Lord.

Rejoice in hope; be patient in affliction; be persistent in prayer. Share with the saints in their needs; pursue hospitality. Bless those who persecute you; bless and do not curse. Rejoice with those who rejoice; weep with those who weep.

Be in agreement with one another. Do not be proud; instead, associate with the humble. Do not be wise in your own estimation. Do not repay anyone evil for evil. Try to do what is honorable in everyone's eyes. If possible, on your part, live at peace with everyone.

Romans 12:9–18

$\mathcal{P}$ractice these things; be committed to them, so that your progress may be evident to all. Be conscientious about yourself and your teaching; persevere in these things, for by doing this you will save both yourself and your hearers.

1 Timothy 4:15–16

*F*or I desire loyalty and not sacrifice,
the knowledge of God
rather than burnt offerings.

Hosea 6:6

*Y*ou do not want a sacrifice,
or I would give it;
You are not pleased with a burnt offering.
The sacrifice pleasing to God is a broken spirit.
God, You will not despise
a broken and humbled heart.

Psalm 51:16–17

*H*ave not our suspicious hearts
darkened this Book of light? Do we not
often read it as the proclamation of a
command to do, instead of a declaration
of what the love of God has done?

—Horatio Bonar

67

For this reason also, since the day we heard this, we haven't stopped praying for you.

We are asking that you may be filled with the knowledge of His will in all wisdom and spiritual understanding, so that you may walk worthy of the Lord, fully pleasing to Him, bearing fruit in every good work and growing in the knowledge of God. May you be strengthened with all power, according to His glorious might, for all endurance and patience, with joy giving thanks to the Father, who has enabled you to share in the saints' inheritance in the light.

He has rescued us from the domain of darkness and transferred us into the kingdom of the Son He loves, in whom we have redemption, the forgiveness of sins.

Colossians 1:9–14

*J*ust as I have loved you, you should also love one another. By this all people will know that you are My disciples, if you have love for one another.

John 13:34b–35

*W*hich commandment is the most important of all?"

"This is the most important," Jesus answered: " 'Hear, O Israel! The Lord our God is one Lord. And you shall love the Lord your God with all your heart, with all your soul, with all your mind, and with all your strength.' The second is: 'You shall love your neighbor as yourself.' There is no other commandment greater than these."

Mark 12:28b–31

*J*esus came into the world to save sinners— and I am the worst of them. But I received mercy because of this, so that in me, the worst of them, Christ Jesus might demonstrate the utmost patience as an example to those who would believe in Him for eternal life.

1 Timothy 1:15b–16

Busyness

God, hear my cry;
pay attention to my prayer.
I call to You from the ends
of the earth when my
heart is without strength.
Lead me to a rock that is
high above me, for You
have been a refuge for me,
a strong tower in the face
of the enemy.

Psalm 61:1–3

Stop This Thing!

*H*ave you ever ridden one of those barrel spinners at the amusement park—the one with the big wheel in the middle and the seats all around, the one that whips the cars in and around each other, spinning, bobbing, twirling. The colors blur, the music reverbs, your hair blows wildly, and the squeals . . .

I hate that ride.

So why do I find myself hopping back onto it so often? Not at the theme park—(never again, Lord, please!)—but in the non-fantasyland of real life?

And how do I make it stop?

Overwhelmed. That's the word you hear yourself saying.

"I'm just overwhelmed."

"This is so overwhelming."

I don't know about the "whelming" part, but I'm all for the being "over" part, aren't you?

It really is crazy what we do to ourselves.

But although life could probably be a lot more ordered and structured than some of us allow it to be, and although certain unavoidable situations arise that knock even our best laid plans off balance, we probably experience God the best during our seasons of "overwhelming."

I mean, most days our hubbub and humdrum lives communicate precious little to others about the difference Christ makes to us. But set us to spinning with impossible problems, and people can suddenly start seeing the glint of treasure inside these jars of clay—a depth of purity and power that can come only "from God and not from us" (2 Corinthians 4:7). Paul's response to such stress was to "be pleased in weaknesses, in insults, in catastrophes, in persecutions, and in pressures. For when I am weak, then I am strong" (2 Corinthians 12:10).

Physically, you may be operating on perpetual exhaustion. Emotionally, you may be a frayed knot of nerves and numbness. But spiritually, you can be drinking from a well deeper than many of us have ever known—the depths of God's higher purposes, the assurance that he knows what he's doing, that he's strengthening the muscles you'll need for perhaps even more difficult days ahead, that he's infusing you with firsthand experiences that will give your advice an authentic ring to people caught in similar situations. Who knows?

Can you take any comfort during times like these from knowing that God is doing something extraordinary in you?

You've been praying all your life for others to see Jesus in you. He may never be more clearly seen in you than he is right now.

So stand there in the storm, even when it's spinning and whirling like mad. And prepare to be overwhelmed by his sustaining, securing power.

I cry aloud to the LORD;
   I plead aloud to the LORD for mercy.
I pour out my complaint before Him;
   I reveal my trouble to Him.
Although my spirit is weak within me,
   You know my way.

Psalm 142:1–3a

*Y*ou guide me with Your counsel,
   and afterward You will take me up in glory.
Whom do I have in heaven but You?
   And I desire nothing on earth but You.
My flesh and my heart may fail,
   but God is the strength of my heart,
   my portion forever.

Psalm 73:24–26

I love You, LORD, my strength.
The LORD is my rock,
   my fortress, and my deliverer,
   my God, my mountain where I seek refuge,
   my shield and the horn of my salvation,
   my stronghold.

Psalm 18:1–2

*H*as God forgotten to be gracious?
   Has He in anger withheld His compassion? . . .
I will remember the LORD's works;
   yes, I will remember Your ancient wonders.
I will reflect on all You have done
   and meditate on Your actions. . . .
You are the God who works wonders;
   You revealed Your strength among the people.

Psalm 77:9, 11–12, 14

O God, You are my God;
   I eagerly seek You.
My soul thirsts for You;
   my body faints for You in a land
   that is dry, desolate, and without water.
So I gaze on You in the sanctuary
   to see Your strength and Your glory.
My lips will glorify You because
   Your faithful love is better than life.
So I will praise You as long as I live;
   at Your name, I will lift up my hands.
You satisfy me as with rich food;
   my mouth will praise you with joyful lips.

Psalm 63:1–5

For You, O LORD, are my lamp;
the LORD illuminates my darkness.
With You I can attack a barrier,
and with my God I can leap a wall. . . .
For who is God besides the LORD?
And who is a rock besides our God?
God is my strong refuge;
He makes my way perfect.

2 Samuel 22:29–30, 32–33

The pledged word of God to man is no puffball to break at a touch and scatter into dust. It is iron. It is gold, the most malleable of metals. It is more golden than gold. It abides imperishable forever.

–Amy Carmichael

*F*inally, be strengthened by the Lord and by His vast strength. Put on the full armor of God so that you can stand against the tactics of the Devil.

For our battle is not against flesh and blood, but against the rulers, against the authorities, against the world powers of this darkness, against the spiritual forces of evil in the heavens.

This is why you must take up the full armor of God, so that you may be able to resist in the evil day, and having prepared everything, to take your stand. . . .

In every situation take the shield of faith, and with it you will be able to extinguish the flaming arrows of the evil one. Take the helmet of salvation, and the sword of the Spirit, which is God's word.

Ephesians 6:10–13, 16–17

For although we are walking in the flesh, we do not wage war in a fleshly way, since the weapons of our warfare are not fleshly, but are powerful through God for the demolition of strongholds. We demolish arguments and every high-minded thing that is raised up against the knowledge of God, taking every thought captive to the obedience of Christ.

2 Corinthians 10:4–5

Do not fear, for I have redeemed you; I have called you by your name; you are Mine. I will be with you when you pass through the waters, and when you pass through the rivers, they will not overwhelm you. You will not be burned when you walk through the fire, and the flame will not burn you. For I am the LORD your God, the Holy One of Israel, your Savior."

Isaiah 43:1b–3a

When you walk,
    your steps will not be hindered;
when you run, you will not stumble.

Proverbs 4:12

Frustration

*W*hy do you assert: "My way is hidden from the LORD, and my claim is ignored by my God"? Do you not know? Have you not heard? The LORD is the everlasting God, the Creator of the earth from end to end. He never grows faint or weary; there is no limit to His understanding. He gives strength to the weary, and strengthens the powerless.

Isaiah 40:27b–29

Why Me? Why Now?

*Y*our husband locked his keys in the car at work, and that means you're going to have to refigure your schedule and make an extra trip into town.

Your son went off to school without his science book . . . (again) . . . so unless you decide it's finally time for him to learn his lesson, you can forget about squeezing in your walk this morning.

Your boss showed up at a 9:00 a.m. meeting, not just to go over the proposal you've been working on, but also to tell you that the client wants to see it this afternoon instead of next Wednesday. No lunch for you today.

Your friend was supposed to meet you for dinner tonight, but there's no answer at her house, nothing but voice mail on her cell phone, and both your iced tea and your impatient server are getting warmer by the minute.

We all know how it feels to be frustrated, to have our day basically figured out, only to find it spoiled and rewritten before we've even had a chance to start it good.

We know the boiling sensation that begins to fume and sizzle about two inches below our necklines, that "I'm gonna get somebody" temptation we thought we'd learned how to control already.

That's our "self" talking. And we can expect to get an earful . . . because as apologetic or demanding or forgetful as others can be, nothing compares to the tone our inner spirits can use when we've been pushed aside, thrown off kilter, or generally jerked around.

We may not always voice our frustrations out loud where everyone can listen, but we can certainly hear them inside of us, pounding up and down the corridors of our hearts—banging pots and pans, ranting and raving, throwing things.

It's ugly.

But it's who we are—and it's who we'll always be unless we take the hard step of denying ourselves, of choosing to serve and surrender with a glad heart.

It really is a choice—a brave decision to not let life steal our joy, to not sacrifice the rewards of unselfish giving by doing it with a sigh and a sneer and a slap on the dashboard.

Life can be frustrating—even the *Christian* life perhaps even more so, because we believers easily become disgusted and disappointed with ourselves, knowing how far we often miss the mark.

How much more freeing and fulfilling our lives would be if we chose to give before anyone asked, if we responded to inconvenience with a smile and an understanding pat on the shoulder, if we did without and didn't feel deprived, if we forgave ourselves and received the fresh start of repentance.

We'll never have this problem totally licked this side of heaven. But we can be sure we'll have lots of practice.

And we can find out how faith stays graceful in the face of frustration.

*D*ear friends, when the fiery ordeal arises among you to test you, don't be surprised by it, as if something unusual were happening to you. Instead, as you share in the sufferings of the Messiah rejoice, so that you may also rejoice with great joy at the revelation of His glory.

1 Peter 4:12–13

*C*onsider it a great joy, my brothers, whenever you experience various trials, knowing that the testing of your faith produces endurance. But endurance must do its complete work, so that you may be mature and complete, lacking nothing.

James 1:2–4

*T*herefore, brothers, by the mercies of God, I urge you to present your bodies as a living sacrifice, holy and pleasing to God; this is your spiritual worship. Do not be conformed to this age, but be transformed by the renewing of your mind, so that you may discern what is the good, pleasing, and perfect will of God.

Romans 12:1–2

You know that those who are regarded as rulers of the Gentiles dominate them, and their men of high positions exercise power over them. But it must not be like that among you.

On the contrary, whoever wants to become great among you must be your servant, and whoever wants to be first among you must be a slave to all. For even the Son of Man did not come to be served, but to serve, and to give His life—a ransom for many.

Mark 10:42–45

The one who loves his life will lose it, and the one who hates his life in this world will keep it for eternal life.

John 12:25

If anyone wants to come with Me, he must deny himself, take up his cross daily, and follow Me. For whoever wants to save his life will lose it, but whoever loses his life because of Me will save it.

Luke 9:23–24

Carry one another's burdens; in this way you will fulfill the law of Christ. For if anyone considers himself to be something when he is nothing, he is deceiving himself. But each person should examine his own work, and then he will have a reason for boasting in himself alone, and not in respect to someone else. For each person will have to carry his own load.

Galatians 6:2–5

The Bible reveals God's soul to us in a way that no other book is able to do. It is a gospel tract, distilling the essence of our relationship to the Lord, but it is also an epic, introducing us to the immensity of an eternal God.

–Joni Eareckson Tada

I raise my eyes toward the mountains.
   Where will my help come from?
My help comes from the LORD,
   the Maker of heaven and earth.
He will not allow your foot to slip;
   your Protector will not slumber.
Indeed, the Protector of Israel
   does not slumber or sleep.
The LORD protects you;
   the LORD is a shelter right by your side.
The sun will not strike you by day,
   or the moon by night.
The LORD will protect you from all harm;
   He will protect your life.
The LORD will protect your coming and going
   both now and forever.

Psalm 121:1–8

If our hearts do not condemn us, we have confidence before God, and can receive whatever we ask from Him because we keep His commands and do what is pleasing in His sight.

Now this is His command: that we believe in the name of His Son Jesus Christ, and love one another as He commanded us. The one who keeps His commands remains in Him, and He in him. And the way we know that He remains in us is from the Spirit He has given us.

1 John 3:21–24

For me, living is Christ.

Philippians 1:21a

So don't worry, saying, 'What will we eat?' or 'What will we drink?' or 'What will we wear?' For the Gentiles eagerly seek all these things, and your heavenly Father knows that you need them. But seek first the kingdom of God and His righteousness, and all these things will be provided for you.

Matthew 6:31–33

Depression

$\mathcal{M}$y soul,
praise the LORD,
and do not forget
all His benefits.
He forgives all your sin;
He heals all your diseases.
He redeems your life
from the Pit;
He crowns you with
love and compassion.
He satisfies you with
goodness; your youth is
renewed like the eagle.

Psalm 103:2–5

Darkness and Light

For some of us, depression may feel like nothing more than being in a bad mood on a bad day. For others it's being in a bad mood on an otherwise good day. For still others it means being incapable of coping with any day.

But very few of us have made it this far in life without experiencing at least a passing wave of depression. Maybe it was mild and it went as fast as it came. Or maybe it took up residence for far too long and continues to make return appearances on a regular basis.

The fact is, we all know a little of what being depressed feels like.

And the interesting part is, so did a lot of the Bible's most famous characters. Elijah certainly did. Cowering in a windswept nowhere land, he begged God to take his life before wicked Jezebel did it for him. For forty days he languished deep in the Middle Eastern wilderness. Troubled, scared, and tired of fighting, Elijah wrestled with a prophet's worst torment— not knowing where to turn, not hearing God's voice, not being sure if he could any longer trust his spiritual senses. Losing all perspective, he gave in to his mind's worst exaggerations, and for a time gave up on everything he had lived for.

Job knew depression too—and for good reason. With his children killed, all his possessions lost, and his health destroyed, he often cried out in contempt to God. We talk about the patience of Job, and his patience does indeed peek its head in from time to time. But we hear a lot more griping and complaining in the book of Job than we do anything else. We hear him saying things like, "I am disgusted with my life. Let me express my complaint and hold nothing back; let me speak out of the bitterness of my soul" (Job 10:1). He was certainly no stranger to deep despair.

King David also experienced it. Several of his psalms describe his suffering in brooding detail, words that sound hauntingly familiar to the way we often feel today. So did Jeremiah, the weeping prophet also known for his book of Lamentations. So did many others, it seems, if you read between the lines and imagine what they must have been feeling.

How kind of God to let us in on this gray side of his saints. How understanding of him to hand down to us so much more than stories of impossible achievement, to also pepper in the woeful writings of strong men and women who weren't immune to losing heart, giving up, or spiraling down.

Yes, some of them were tormented for large portions of their lives with varying degrees of depression. But from our historical perspective, we can look back and see that it didn't define them. Take their lives as a whole, and you'll see that God was bigger than their depression. He used them despite their depression. He brought something good out of their depression.

We may suffer on many days, perhaps most days. But the story of our lives can still be written in terms of God's glory and God's deliverance. We must persevere. We must keep believing. We must not be afraid.

Our God is our refuge.

*W*hy has my pain become unending;
  my wound incurable, refusing to be healed?
You truly have become like a mirage to me,
  water that is not reliable.

Jeremiah 15:18

*Y*ou have distanced loved one and neighbor
  from me; darkness is my only friend.

Psalm 88:18

*D*o not rejoice over me, my enemy!
  Though I have fallen, I will stand up.
Though I sit in darkness,
  the LORD will be my light.

Micah 7:8

*F*or He will not reject forever,
  the LORD, that is.
Even if He torments,
  He will show compassion,
  according to His abundant faithful love.
For He does not afflict capriciously
  nor abuse the human race.

Lamentations 3:31–33

The ropes of death were wrapped around me,
and the torments of Sheol overcame me;
I encountered trouble and sorrow.
Then I called on the name of the LORD:
"LORD, save me!"
The LORD is gracious and righteous;
our God is compassionate.
The LORD guards the inexperienced;
I was helpless, and He saved me.
Return to your rest, my soul,
for the LORD has been good to you.
For You, LORD, rescued me from death,
my eyes from tears, my feet from stumbling.
I will walk before the LORD
in the land of the living.
I believed, even when I said,
"I am severely afflicted."
In my alarm I said, "Everyone is a liar."
How can I repay the LORD
all the good He has done for me?
I will take the cup of salvation
and worship the LORD.
I will fulfill my vows to the LORD
in the presence of all His people.

Psalm 116:3–14

*I*n that day I will respond,
  declares the LORD. . . .
I will sow her in the land for Myself,
  and I will pity "Not-Pitied";
I will say to "Not-My-People,"
  "You are My people!"
  and he will say, "My God!"

Hosea 2:21a, 23

*G*od's Word has sustained me. There

have been times when I have only been

capable of reading a few verses at a time,

yet the supernatural, life-giving power of

the Word of God has given me strength

to go on, even if only one day at a time.

–Anne Graham Lotz

The waters engulfed me up to the neck;
  the watery depths overcame me. . . .
I sank to the foundations of the mountains;
  the earth with its prison bars
  closed behind me forever!
But You raised my life from the pit,
  O LORD my God!
As my life was fading away,
  I remembered the LORD.
My prayer came to You,
  to Your holy temple.
Those who cling to worthless idols
  forsake faithful love;
  but as for me, I will sacrifice to You
  with a voice of thanksgiving.
I will fulfill what I have vowed.
  Salvation is from the LORD!

Jonah 2:5a, 6–9

Lord, my every desire is known to You;
my sighing is not hidden from You.

Psalm 38:9

I have asked one thing from the LORD;
it is what I desire: to dwell in the house
of the LORD all the days of my life,
gazing on the beauty of the LORD
and seeking Him in His temple.
For He will conceal me in His shelter
in the day of adversity;
He will hide me under the cover of His tent;
He will set me high on a rock.
Then my head will be high above my enemies
around me; I will offer sacrifices
in His tent with shouts of joy.
I will sing and make music to the LORD.

Psalm 27:4–6

For God has not given us a spirit of fear-
fulness, but one of power, love, and sound
judgment.

2 Timothy 1:7

*W*ho perceives his unintentional sins? Cleanse me from my hidden faults. Moreover, keep Your servant from willful sins; do not let them rule over me. . . . May the words of my mouth and the meditation of my heart be acceptable to You, O LORD, my rock and my Redeemer.

Psalm 19:12–13a, 14

What's So Good About It?

*I*n the classic children's story *Grumley the Grouch*, an overly touchy mole named Grumley is constantly irritating his friends with his pervading unhappiness . . . and his unapologetic freedom in sharing it around. Always displeased, always uncomfortable, always out of sorts with his neighbors and acquaintances, he lives in a perpetual state between anger and displeasure.

When asked why he chooses to remain in such a sorry state, why he persists at being short-fused and cantankerous, why he can't bring himself to find *something—anything*—to like in the world, he sneeringly responds, "Well, there's so much not to like."

Can't argue with him there. If all we had to go on were the dirty socks and distasteful habits of the people we must share our lives with, then we could easily conclude that there's not always much to like in our average day. We have people who mistreat us, people who ignore us, people who undermine us, people who annoy us. We have friends at church who *ask* too much, neighbors next door who *snoop* too much, supervisors at work who *demand* too much, and cashiers at the grocery store who *talk* too much (to the cute bagboys, mostly). And we haven't even gotten *home* yet! (They'd better not push it!)

It just makes us mad. Not always a furious, raise-your-voice mad, but just sort of a simmering, leave-me-alone mad. We become hard to live with, hard to accommodate, hard to please.

Hard to see Jesus in.

Yet much of what angers us can't be replaced or exchanged. Even if we were somehow able to peel away some of our stressors and flashpoints, they would only be substituted by others, different but no less subject to our eventual dismay.

It basically boils back down to us.

Lord, will you help us not be so quick in finding fault with others? Will you help us not so easily feel put upon when someone asks us to do something for them? Will you help us be slower to assume the worst in people, more patient with temporary inconveniences, and more free to show love and graciousness when we'd just as soon bite someone's head off?

Of course he will.

Grumley finally met in his match in the story— a female mole just as ornery and discontent as he was. For a while they merely enjoyed each other's misery, but over time they came to discover that anger and ill-temperedness can be replaced by patience and optimism. Life that seemed so unlikable wasn't really as dark and cloudy as it seemed, they discovered. It was all in the way they looked at it.

Yes, it's all in the way we look at it.

Refrain from anger and give up your rage;
do not be agitated—it can only bring harm.

Psalm 37:8

Be angry and do not sin. Don't let the
sun go down on your anger, and don't give the
Devil an opportunity.

Ephesians 4:26–27

For it is God's will that you, by doing
good, silence the ignorance of foolish people.

1 Peter 2:15

A gentle answer turns away anger,
but a harsh word stirs up wrath.

Proverbs 15:1

Understand this: everyone must be quick to
hear, slow to speak, and slow to anger, for man's
anger does not accomplish God's righteousness.

James 1:19–20

ℰach one of us must please his neighbor for his good, in order to build him up.

For even the Messiah did not please Himself. On the contrary, as it is written, "The insults of those who insult You have fallen on Me."

Romans 15:2–3

𝒯herefore, God's chosen ones, holy and loved, put on heartfelt compassion, kindness, humility, gentleness, and patience, accepting one another and forgiving one another if anyone has a complaint against another. Just as the Lord has forgiven you, so also you must forgive.

Above all, put on love—the perfect bond of unity. And let the peace of the Messiah, to which you were also called in one body, control your hearts. Be thankful.

Let the message about the Messiah dwell richly among you, teaching and admonishing one another in all wisdom, and singing psalms, hymns, and spiritual songs, with gratitude in your hearts to God.

Colossians 3:12–16

*A*nd whatever you do, in word or in deed, do everything in the name of the Lord Jesus, giving thanks to God the Father through Him.

Colossians 3:17

*S*peak and act as those who will be judged by the law of freedom. For judgment is without mercy to the one who hasn't shown mercy. Mercy triumphs over judgment.

James 2:12–13

It has been well said that upsetting the Bible is like upsetting a solid cube of granite; it is just as big one way as the other, and when you have upset it, it is right side up, and when you overturn it again, it is right side up still.

–David F. Nygren

I say to you who listen: Love your enemies, do good to those who hate you, bless those who curse you, pray for those who mistreat you.

If anyone hits you on the cheek, offer the other also. And if anyone takes away your coat, don't hold back your shirt either. Give to everyone who asks from you, and from one who takes away your things, don't ask for them back. Just as you want others to do for you, do the same for them.

If you love those who love you, what credit is that to you? Even sinners love those who love them. If you do good to those who do good to you, what credit is that to you? Even sinners do that. . . . But love your enemies, do good, and lend, expecting nothing in return. Then your reward will be great.

Luke 6:27–33, 35a

$\mathscr{N}$ow finally, all of you should be like-minded and sympathetic, should love believers, and be compassionate and humble, not paying back evil for evil or insult for insult but, on the contrary, giving a blessing, since you were called for this, so that you can inherit a blessing.

1 Peter 3:8–9

$\mathscr{N}$o rotten talk should come from your mouth, but only what is good for the building up of someone in need, in order to give grace to those who hear. . . . All bitterness, anger and wrath, insult and slander must be removed from you, along with all wickedness. And be kind and compassionate to one another, forgiving one another, just as God also forgave you in Christ.

Ephesians 4:29, 31–32

$\mathscr{N}$ow may the God of endurance and encouragement grant you agreement with one another, according to Christ Jesus, so that you may glorify the God and Father of our Lord Jesus Christ with a united mind and voice.

Romans 15:5–6

I will give you a new heart and I will put a new spirit within you. I will remove the heart of stone from your flesh and give you a heart of flesh. I will put my spirit within you and make you walk in My statutes and you will keep My judgments diligently.

Ezekiel 36:26–27

If I Had It to Do Over

$\mathcal{W}$e take so much of our life experience for granted, as though God could never have chosen to do things differently than he did. For example, he didn't have to build into us the ability to remember. Can you imagine how odd and restrictive that would be—to only be able to have awareness of the present? No anticipation of the future? No memories?

Oh, memory is a wonderful blessing. It helps us continue to see the faces of those we love who have left us in death. Through memory we can still hear their laugh, recognize their gestures, and pick them out in our stories.

Memory helps us spot patterns in life, reminding us of a course of action we once took in a similar situation, allowing us to make each new decision with a bit of a head start, a base level of knowledge and understanding we can build on and refer to.

Memory connects us in time with people we may have never met before this morning, yet with whom we somehow share a whole world of common events. It's the one human ability that can turn a particular aroma, or a certain phrase, or some offhand observation into an immediate flashback, transporting our thoughts back a year, or a decade, or a lifetime.

But in order to enjoy this tremendous blessing, we must also be willing for our memory to be honest. Not all memories are of Sunday afternoon dinners at our grandparents' house, or of summer youth retreats with our church group, or of family vacations to the beach or the lake cabin or the mountains.

Some memories hurt. Some memories we'd like to forget. And my, how the devil enjoys making that hard to do.

Yes, we've made our fair share of mistakes . . . and then some. We've been careless with our character. We've been too harsh and unforgiving. We've been oblivious to others' needs even though they were right under our noses.

We've wasted an opportunity here. We've made an accidental error there. We've hurt someone's feelings. We've spoken up when we should have kept quiet. We've been guilty of woeful lapses in judgment.

We've stepped out of our gifting area and paid the price for trying to be everything to everybody. We've harped on a certain flaw in our children's demeanor and failed to encourage their traits that are worthy of praise. We've spent money we didn't have and now we have payments we can't afford.

Or worse.

And yet there is no memory—however grim and unbearable—that doesn't have some sense of God's deliverance around it. Even in our worst moments, God has been there to rescue and restore, to turn our messes into monuments of his mercy.

So let's not allow the devil to turn God's gift of memory into a horror show that keeps us up nights, making us unable to sleep for the things we've seen and heard. Instead, let's thank God for the memory of his faithfulness, and cherish the One who can make all things new.

Blessed are the poor in spirit,
  because the kingdom of heaven is theirs.
Blessed are those who mourn,
  because they will be comforted.
Blessed are the gentle,
  because they will inherit the earth.

Matthew 5:3–5

LORD, if You considered sins,
  Lord, who could stand?
But with You there is forgiveness,
  so that You may be revered.
I wait for the LORD; I wait,
  and put my hope in His word.
I wait for the Lord
  more than watchmen for the morning—
  more than watchmen for the morning.

Psalm 130:3–6

That is how we will know we are of the truth, and will convince our hearts in His presence, because if our hearts condemn us, God is greater than our hearts and knows all things.

1 John 3:19–20

$\mathcal{S}$ay to the faint-hearted:
  "Be strong; do not fear!
Here is your God; vengeance is coming.
  God's retribution is coming;
  He will save you!". . .
Then the lame will leap like a deer,
  and the tongue of the mute will sing for joy,
  for water will gush in the wilderness,
  and streams in the desert; the parched
  ground will become a pool of water,
  and the thirsty land springs of water. . . .
A road will be there and a way;
  it will be called the Holy Way.
The unclean will not travel on it,
  but it will be for him who walks the path.
  Even the fool will not go astray. . . .
But the redeemed will walk on it,
  and the ransomed of the LORD will return
  and come to Zion with singing,
  crowned with unending joy.
Joy and gladness will overtake them,
  and sorrow and groaning will disappear.
                    Isaiah 35:4, 6–7a, 8, 9b–10

$\mathcal{G}$odly grief produces a repentance not to be regretted and leading to salvation. . . . For consider how much diligence this very thing—this grieving as God wills—has produced in you: what a desire to clear yourselves, what indignation, what fear, what deep longing, what zeal, what justice! In every way you have commended yourselves to be pure in this matter.

2 Corinthians 7:10a, 11

To know and embrace and live by
God's Word is to know and embrace
and live by Him; it is to build that
solid, unshakable structure that will
keep you from collapsing in the rubble
of disappointment's earthquakes.

–Kay Arthur

*Y*ou have said: "Surely our transgressions and our sins are upon us and on account of them we are wasting away. How then can we live?"

Say to them, "As I live," declares the Lord GOD, 'I do not delight in the death of a wicked person, but rather that the wicked person turn from his way and live. . . ."

Likewise, when I say to the wicked person "You shall surely die," and he turns from his sin and does what is just and right—when the wicked person returns collateral and makes restitution for what he has stolen, and walks in the statutes of life, so as not to commit evil— he will of course live; he will not die. None of the sins that he committed will be remembered against him.

He has done what is just and right; he will of course live.

Ezekiel 33:10b–11a, 14–16

As a mother comforts her son,
  so I will comfort you;
  and you will be comforted in Jerusalem.

Isaiah 66:13

I greatly rejoice in the LORD,
  I exult in my God;
  for He has clothed me
  with the garments of salvation
  and wrapped me
  in a robe of righteousness,
  as a bridegroom wearing a turban,
  and as a bride adorned with her jewels.

Isaiah 61:10

Go and eat what is rich, drink what is sweet, and send portions to those who have nothing prepared, for today is holy to our LORD. Do not grieve, for rejoicing in the LORD is your fortress.

Nehemiah 8:10

Prayer

$\mathcal{L}$et me experience Your faithful love in the morning, for I trust in You. Reveal to me the way I should go, because I long for You. Rescue me from my enemies, LORD; I come to You for protection. Teach me to do Your will, for You are my God. May Your gracious Spirit lead me on level ground.

Psalm 143:8–10

What Do You Need?

*W*hen was the last time you started out in prayer and ended up just talking to yourself?

Or am I the only one who does that?

Why do we do that? It's probably because we're too often trying to pray while we're busy doing something else—like driving the car or making sandwiches. Not that there's anything wrong—in fact, there's everything *right*—about talking with God while we're in the middle of a common task. But if that's the *only* time we ever find to visit with him, we're going to always end up in this disjointed little spin cycle, slipping in and out between prayer and more pressing matters.

Jim Cymbala, pastor of the Brooklyn Tabernacle and author of the best-selling book *Fresh Wind, Fresh Fire*, writes about their church's Tuesday night prayer meetings. The stories that have come from this weekly gathering are unbelievable—lines of people stringing out into the street, hoping to find a place to sit in the capacity-filled auditorium, expecting to meet with God and experience his presence along with this vibrant body of believers. The needs are dire. The spiritual atmosphere is electric. The answers to prayer are amazing.

Many have been inspired by this intriguing idea, wanting to bring it back to their own churches as a model for the way prayer ought to be done in their congregations. Good. They should. But it's not Tuesday night that makes it special. It's not magical just because it works in one of the most dynamic cities in the world. Jim Cymbala is quick to point out that their church doesn't pray together on Tuesday nights because they think it's a cool idea.

They pray because they have to.

They pray because they have no other choice.

And that's the one basic thing that keeps us from praying like we should: we don't really think we need to. That's why we so often insert our only prayers of the day among things like doing the laundry or sweeping the front porch . . . if in fact we even work prayer into our day at all. That's why we sleep in until the last minute and leave no time for God in our morning routine. That's why we find ourselves feeling so distant and awkward when we arrive at a situation where we desperately need God, when we have to call his 911 number even though it's the first time we've spoken in weeks.

Oh, I'm not meaning to be overly heavy here. I share your struggle at not always seeing the sense in prayer. But the frame of mind and spirit that keeps us from recognizing our need for time with God is an outright lie disguised in a busy lifestyle.

We desperately need him.

We need to hear him.

We need to be near him.

We need to pray.

*N*ow this is the confidence we have before Him: whenever we ask anything according to His will, He hears us. And if we know that He hears whatever we ask, we know that we have what we have asked Him for.

1 John 5:14–15

*K*eep asking, and it will be given to you. Keep searching, and you will find. Keep knocking, and the door will be opened to you.

Matthew 7:7

*W*hen you pray, don't babble like the idolaters, since they imagine they'll be heard for their many words. Don't be like them, because your Father knows the things you need before you ask Him.

Matthew 6:7–8

*T*herefore let us approach the throne of grace with boldness, so that we may receive mercy and find grace to help us at the proper time.

Hebrews 4:16

$\mathcal{I}$ cry aloud to God,
  aloud to God, and He will hear me.
In my day of trouble I sought the Lord.
  My hands were lifted up all night long.
Psalm 77:1–2a

$\mathcal{T}$he LORD is near all who call out to Him,
  all who call out to Him with integrity.
He fulfills the desires of those who fear Him;
  He hears their cry for help and saves them.
Psalm 145:18–19

$\mathcal{Y}$ou will petition Him, and He will hear you,
  while you pay what you promised under oath.
You will make a decision
  and it will be done for you.
Light will shine on your ways.
Job 22:27–28

$\mathcal{B}$e gracious to me, Lord,
  for I call to You all day long. . . .
For You, Lord, are kind and ready to forgive,
  abundant in faithful love to all who call on You.
Psalm 86:3, 5

May the name of God
  be praised forever and ever,
  for wisdom and power belong to Him.
He changes the times and seasons;
  He removes kings and establishes kings.
He gives wisdom to the wise
  and knowledge to those
  who have understanding.
He reveals the deep and hidden things.

Daniel 2:20–22a

God has handed us two sticks of dynamite with which to demolish our strongholds: His Word and prayer. What is more powerful than two sticks of dynamite placed in separate locations? Two strapped together.

—Beth Moore

$\mathcal{C}$ome and see the works of God;
His acts toward mankind
are awe-inspiring. . . .
Come and listen, all who fear God,
and I will tell what He has done for me.
I cried out to Him with my mouth,
and praise was on my tongue.
If I had been aware of malice in my heart,
the Lord would not have listened.
However, God has listened;
He has paid attention
to the sound of my prayer.
May God be praised!
He has not turned away my prayer
or turned His faithful love from me.

Psalm 66:5, 16–20

*N*ow if any of you lacks wisdom, he
should ask God, who gives to all generously and
without criticizing, and it will be given to him.

James 1:5

*E*ven before they call, I will answer;
while they are still speaking,
I will hear.

Isaiah 65:24

*L*ORD my God,
You have done many things—
Your wonderful works and Your plans for us;
none can compare with You.
If I were to report and speak of them,
they are more than can be told.

Psalm 40:5

*B*ut as for me, I will watch for the LORD;
I will wait for the God who saves me.
My God will hear me.

Micah 7:7

$\mathcal{L}$ook at how great a love the Father has given us, that we should be called God's children. And we are! Dear friends, we are God's children now, and what we will be has not yet been revealed. We know that when He appears, we will be like Him, because we will see Him as He is. And everyone who has this hope in Him purifies himself just as He is pure.

1 John 3:1a, 2–3

Somebody Loves You

*L*ove is easier for some of us to accept than it is for others.

But in the will of God and in the person of Jesus Christ, love has been poured out on us whether we were comfortable receiving it or not.

Poured out like a river cascading over a waterfall, crashing with unrelenting power into our thirsty hearts, erupting into a steamy mist that saturates us through and through, soaking our renewed spirits in unrestrained refreshment.

Lavished upon us like riches strewn in handfuls across the table in front of us, our eyes widened in surprise at the invitation to come and buy what our hearts never dreamed really existed—lasting joy, abiding peace, eternal life and security.

Flung like a dancing field of gold and violet wildflowers, waving gently in a spring breeze, heads held high to drink in the sun that beams from a turquoise sky and flushes the face of young girl, her shoes giving way to bare feet and the carpeted luxury of a clovered countryside.

We can't really grasp how much God loves us.

One day in heaven we'll be able to describe it. We'll sit down with pen in hand, perhaps, replacing the words that always seemed so inadequate on earth with terms and phrases that not only say it right but sing it in rhythm.

And then we'll start to understand. Then we'll start to get our minds around it—though something tells me that even then, we'll never totally lose our speechlessness at what God has done for us.

Have you received his love today?

Has he already made you aware that your sins no longer need to stand in the way between you and his promises?

Has he shown you how you can repent of your sins—to turn away from them, never to return—and how to receive his full and forever forgiveness?

Has he made clear that you can believe in him—believe in Jesus Christ's sinless life, his death on the cross as the full payment on your debt, his resurrection from the dead as your hope of eternal victory?

Has he painted for you the picture of a home in heaven—a literal place more real than the earth we've grown so accustomed to, a place to which he's gone to prepare a place for you and for all those who long for and await his soon appearing?

Have you welcomed Jesus Christ into the throneroom of your heart—to be the Savior of your soul and the Lord of your life?

What love he has given us!

What joy he has promised us!

What life he has provided us!

What a wonder our Jesus is!

$\mathcal{R}$arely will someone die for a just person —though for a good person perhaps someone might even dare to die. But God proves His own love for us in that while we were still sinners Christ died for us!

Romans 5:6–8

$\mathcal{N}$o one has greater love than this, that someone would lay down his life for his friends.

John 15:13

$\mathcal{A}$nd we have come to know and to believe the love that God has for us. God is love, and the one who remains in love remains in God, and God remains in him.

In this, love is perfected with us so that we may have confidence in the day of judgment; for we are as He is in this world.

There is no fear in love; instead, perfect love drives out fear, because fear involves punishment. So the one who fears has not reached perfection in love.

We love because He first loved us.

1 John 4:16–19

$\mathcal{L}$ove consists in this: not that we loved God, but that He loved us and sent His Son to be the propitiation for our sins.

Dear friends, if God loved us in this way, we also must love one another.

No one has ever seen God. If we love one another, God remains in us and His love is perfected in us.

1 John 4:9–12

$\mathcal{A}$ren't two sparrows sold for a penny? Yet not one of them falls to the ground without your Father's consent. But even the hairs of your head have all been counted. Don't be afraid therefore; you are worth more than many sparrows.

Matthew 10:29–31

$\mathcal{Y}$ou did not choose Me, but I chose you. I appointed you that you should go out and produce fruit, and that your fruit should remain, so that whatever you ask the Father in My name, He will give you.

John 15:16

For if, while we were enemies, we were reconciled to God through the death of His Son, then how much more, having been reconciled, will we be saved by His life! And not only that, but we also rejoice in God through our Lord Jesus Christ, through whom we have now received reconciliation.

Romans 5:10–11

To Him who loves us and has set us free from our sins by His blood, and made us a kingdom, priests to His God and Father—to Him be the glory and dominion forever and ever.

Revelation 1:5b–6

The Scriptures were not given to us

that we should enclose them in books,

but engrave them upon our hearts.

–John Chrysostom

*W*ho can separate us
from the love of Christ?
Can affliction or anguish
or persecution or famine
or nakedness or danger or sword? . . .
No, in all these things
we are more than victorious
through Him who loved us.
For I am persuaded
that neither death nor life,
nor angels nor rulers,
nor things present, nor things to come,
nor powers, nor height, nor depth,
nor any other created thing
will have the power to separate us
from the love of God that is in
Christ Jesus our Lord!

Romans 8:35, 37–39

I have been crucified with Christ; and I no longer live, but Christ lives in me. The life I now live in the flesh, I live by faith in the Son of God, who loved me and gave Himself for me.

Galatians 2:19b–20

He also raised us up with Him and seated us with Him in the heavens, in Christ Jesus, so that in the coming ages He might display the immeasurable riches of His grace in His kindness to us in Christ Jesus.

Ephesians 2:6–7

But whoever keeps His word, truly in him the love of God is perfected. This is how we know we are in Him: the one who says he remains in Him should walk just as He walked.

1 John 2:5–6

To those who are the called, loved by God the Father and kept by Jesus Christ. May mercy, peace, and love be multiplied to you.

Jude 1b–2

Praise

ℋow unsearchable
His judgments and
untraceable His ways!
For who has known
the mind of the Lord?
Or who has been His
counselor? Or who has
ever first given to Him,
and has to be repaid?
For from Him and
through Him and to
Him are all things.

Romans 11:33b–36a

The Sound of Our Praise

The church today is locked in a worship war.

Some people prefer the sacred hymns, the old standards of the faith, so rich in lyric and composition, so steady and stalwart, so familiar and full of faith.

Some people prefer the newer stuff, the simple songs and choruses, the upbeat sounds of drum and guitar, the hands unafraid to clap their praise.

Some prefer a mixture, a healthy balance. Some prefer a worship even more solemn or far out than either of these.

Have you ever thought about it this way, though? Have you ever considered the possibility that on any given Sunday morning, while a 200-year-old downtown church in a small rural town is "Standing on the

Promises" and "Leaning on the Everlasting Arms," and while a big-city suburban church is standing in the aisles and leaning into the beat, God may be taking both of these worship offerings into his ears—and basking in the symphony of his people's praise?

You know what it's like when all the parts of the symphony are playing together—the strings soaring high and dipping low, the brass instruments peppering the melody with polished counterpoints, the woodwinds adding both their lilts and laments, the percussion pounding out the rhythm and surprising with an occasional ring-off or sound effect.

It's beautiful.

But not because one section is drowning out another.

Not because the violins are a little more musical than the flute or the flugelhorn.

The reason it's beautiful is because it takes all of them to create a complete musical experience.

And perhaps it takes all of God's people, offering up all kinds of different musical styles and languages, to make God truly happy on a typical Sunday morning.

Perhaps.

But certainly we all should want nothing more than for our worship to come purely from our hearts, to be intended purely for his enjoyment and glory. Certainly we should all think less about what kind of an impression our worship might make on the row of weekly visitors, and we should think more about what kind of impression the Lord is receiving from our praise.

For as long as he is pleased, we should all be pleased.

As long as he is made welcome, we should all feel at home in his presence.

As long as he is praised, we should all be willing to play our part in his symphony.

And sing!

Come, let us worship and bow down;
let us kneel before the LORD our Maker.
For He is our God, and we are the people
of His pasture, the sheep under His care.

Psalm 95:6–7

For You are my hope, Lord GOD,
my confidence from my youth.
I have leaned on You from birth;
You took me from my mother's womb.
My praise is always about You.

Psalm 71:5–6

Better a day in Your courts
than a thousand anywhere else.
I would rather be at the door of the house of my
God than to live in the tents of the wicked.
For the LORD God is a sun and shield.
The LORD gives grace and glory;
He does not withhold the good
from those who live with integrity.
LORD of Hosts,
happy is the person who trusts in You!

Psalm 84:10–12

Lord, You are my portion
   and my cup of blessing; You hold my future.
The boundary lines
   have fallen for me in pleasant places;
   indeed, I have a beautiful inheritance.

Psalm 16:5–6

For here we do not have an enduring
city; instead, we seek the one to come.
Therefore, through Him let us continually
offer up to God a sacrifice of praise, that is,
the fruit of our lips that confess His name.

Hebrews 13:14–15

Sing to the Lord,
   for He has done glorious things.
   Let this be known throughout the earth.

Isaiah 12:5

I will sing about
   the Lord's faithful love forever;
   with my mouth I will proclaim
   Your faithfulness to all generations.

Psalm 89:1

You have a mighty arm;
Your hand is powerful;
   Your right hand is lifted high.
Righteousness and justice
   are the foundation of Your throne;
   faithful love and truth go before You.
Happy are the people
   who know the joyful shout;
   LORD, they walk in the light of Your presence.
They rejoice in Your name all day long,
   and they are exalted by Your righteousness.
For You are their magnificent strength.

Psalm 89:13–17a

Scripture is not a concept; Scripture is a person. When you stand before the Word of God, you are standing face-to-face with God.

—Henry Blackaby

*B*lessed be the God and Father of our Lord Jesus Christ.

According to His great mercy, He has given us a new birth into a living hope through the resurrection of Jesus Christ from the dead, and into an inheritance that is imperishable, uncorrupted, and unfading, kept in heaven for you, who are being protected by God's power through faith for a salvation that is ready to be revealed in the last time.

You rejoice in this, though now for a short time you have had to be distressed by various trials so that the genuineness of your faith—more valuable than gold, which perishes though refined by fire—may result in praise, glory, and honor at the revelation of Jesus Christ.

1 Peter 1:3–7

How good it is to sing to our God,
 for praise is pleasant and lovely.

Psalm 147:1

When, on my bed, I think of You,
 I meditate on You during the night watches
 because You are my help;
 I will rejoice in the shadow of Your wings.
I follow close to You;
 Your right hand holds on to me.

Psalm 63:6–8

Those who know Your name trust in You
 because You have not abandoned
 those who seek You, LORD.

Psalm 9:10

My salvation and glory depend on God;
 my strong rock, my refuge, is in God.
Trust in Him at all times, you people;
 pour out your hearts before Him.
 God is our refuge.

Psalm 62:7–8

Gratitude

$\mathcal{L}$et them give
thanks to the LORD
for His faithful love
and His wonderful
works for the human
race. For He has
satisfied the thirsty
and filled the hungry
with good things.

Psalm 107:8–9

Thanks For Everything

A small, scented bead of hand lotion worked smoothly through your fingers.

The flick of goldfish fins.

The convenience of a pocket calculator.

Peppermint plants coming up again in the early summer.

Peanut butter.

The strange, sticky property of water that makes it cling together into droplets instead of whatever odd form it would take if God hadn't made it the way he did.

Pictures of our children on the mantlepiece.

Pencils with a nice, hard, sharp lead (not the ones that make that soft, fat line) and a full, lots-of-life-left push-on eraser.

The Grand Canyon.

Involuntary muscles.

Rainfall about 11 o'clock on a Saturday night . . . and still gently coming down when you wake up and turn over around 3:00 a.m.

Lightning bugs. (God must have had fun coming up with lightning bugs.)

Descriptive adverbs.

Having two full sets of Christian grandmothers and grandfathers.

Okra blooms.

A handwritten letter in the afternoon mail.

Automatic garage door openers.

December.

Movies where people break into song right in the middle of what they were doing.

That new kind of pillow that NASA or somebody invented, the one that sort of remembers the shape of your head and feels like you're laying in a warm bath.

The time of year when ticks and snakes aren't out anymore.

Watching a bunny rabbit get an orange mouth from eating a carrot.

The golden rule.

The color yellow.

Dryer sheets.

Sunday afternoon.

The warm, wafting smell you experience after driving by an industrial bakery.

The fact that two plus two always equals four. Always.

Knowing where the scissors and tape are when you need to wrap a present.

A hair stylist who's easy to talk to—and who almost always cuts your hair right.

Andy Griffith Show reruns.

Vitamin C.

The whispery sound of Bible paper when you're about three pages away from the passage you're searching for.

The chance to answer your child's tooth fairy note.

The lightness in your heart when you've done something kind for someone . . . for no reason.

Ceiling fans.

The warbly sound of a little old lady's singing voice who's sitting behind you in church service.

My, my—there really are a lot of things to be thankful for.

And only one Person to send the thank-you note to.

*L*ord, You have been our refuge
  in every generation.
Before the mountains were born,
  before You gave birth
  to the earth and the world,
  from eternity to eternity, You are God.

Psalm 90:1–2

I remember the days of old;
  I meditate on all You have done;
  I reflect on the work of Your hands.

Psalm 143:5

*I*f Your instruction had not been my delight,
  I would have died in my affliction.
I will never forget Your precepts,
  for You have given me life through them.

Psalm 119:92–93

*O*ur mouths were filled with laughter then,
  and our tongues with shouts of joy.
Then they said among the nations,
  "The LORD has done great things for them."

Psalm 126:2

*B*lessed be the God and Father of our Lord Jesus Christ, who has blessed us with every spiritual blessing in the heavens, in Christ; for He chose us in Him, before the foundation of the world, to be holy and blameless in His sight.

In love He predestined us to be adopted through Jesus Christ for Himself, according to His favor and will, to the praise of His glorious grace that He favored us with in the Beloved.

In Him we have redemption through His blood, the forgiveness of our trespasses, according to the riches of His grace that He lavished on us with all wisdom and understanding.

He made known to us the mystery of His will, according to His good pleasure that He planned in Him for the administration of the days of fulfillment—to bring everything together in the Messiah.

Ephesians 1:3–10a

*F*or God was pleased to have all His fullness dwell in Him, and through Him to reconcile everything to Himself.

Colossians 1:19–20a

But you are a chosen race,
   a royal priesthood,
   a holy nation, a people for His possession,
   so that you may proclaim the praises
   of the One who called you out of
   darkness into His marvelous light.
Once you were not a people,
   but now you are God's people;
   you had not received mercy,
   but now you have received mercy.

1 Peter 2:9–10

Break thou the bread of life, dear
   Lord, to me / As thou didst break the
   loaves beside the sea / Beyond the sacred
   page I seek thee, Lord / My spirit pants
   for thee, O living Word.

—Mary A. Lathbury

*I*f the LORD had not been on our side—
  let Israel say—
If the LORD had not been on our side
  when men attacked us,
    then they would have swallowed us alive
    in their burning anger against us.
Then the waters would have engulfed us;
  the torrent would have swept over us;
  the raging waters would have swept over us.
Praise the LORD,
  who has not let us
  be ripped apart by their teeth.
We have escaped like a bird
  from the hunter's net;
  the net is torn, and we have escaped.
Our help is in the name of the LORD,
  the Maker of heaven and earth.

*Psalm
124:1–8*

$\mathcal{G}$ive thanks in everything, for this is God's will for you in Christ Jesus.

1 Thessalonians 5:18

$\mathcal{I}$ will praise the LORD at all times;
His praise will always be on my lips.
I will boast in the LORD;
the humble will hear and be glad.

Psalm 34:1–2

$\mathcal{G}$ive thanks to the LORD, for He is good;
His faithful love endures forever.
Let the redeemed of the LORD proclaim
that He has redeemed them
from the hand of the foe
and has gathered them from the lands—
from the east and the west,
from the north and the south.

Psalm 107:1–3

$\mathcal{M}$y mouth will tell about
Your righteousness and Your salvation
all day long, though I cannot sum them up.

Psalm 71:15

Then children were brought to Him so He might put His hands on them and pray. But the disciples rebuked them. Then Jesus said, "Leave the children alone, and don't try to keep them from coming to Me, because the kingdom of heaven is made up of people like this."

Matthew 19:13–14

Just Be Yourself

$\mathcal{T}$his is some of the first advice we receive as children—to always be ourselves, to not give other people the permission to define who we are.

But even those who strike it rich from early on in the popularity department must grapple with the temptation to be someone they're not. I don't think anyone ever totally escapes this. There's simply something inside of us—and always a few unwanted physical features *outside* of us— that make us wish we were somebody else.

We're not born being absolutely sure that God did his best work on us.

And most of us tend to still feel that way long after childhood has come and gone.

This final devotional reading of the book is not merely a "believe in yourself" chapter, some kind of plastic appeal for you to think more positively about who you are. It's not an "up with people" campaign.

This is a "praise God" appeal—an invitation for you and me to celebrate what he has done and is doing in our lives.

It's no little matter.

Many people believe that the Christian life is a constant exercise in self-analysis, that we must be relentless in questioning our motives, punishing ourselves for failing to conquer our weaknesses, rooting out the slightest hint of a raised voice, an unkind thought, or a decrease in spiritual passion.

And while it's true that we mustn't tolerate any form of sin in our lives and must give God full permission to transform everything about us in the direction of his will, we can drive ourselves crazy becoming overly introspective. Just about anytime that we spend too much of our attention focusing on ourselves, the result will be discouragement, disappointment, or outright disgust.

That's why the Scriptures teach us to begin and end our assessment of ourselves by looking away to Jesus, by focusing on the love he has shown to us by living and dying for us. In him we see our true identity.

Yes, we see our sins and shortcomings, too. They're real, and they must be surrendered to him in exchange for a better reward—the reward of obedience. But as believers we are no longer defined by our failures and our fallenness. In the eyes of the One who matters most, we are deemed worthy and righteous and holy and blameless.

Make an appointment sometime soon with the pages of Ephesians, chapter one. And read for yourself about the "blessing" and the "good pleasure" of God, who saw in you a trophy of his mercy and grace. You are far from perfect, of course, yet you are daily yielding to his transforming power, chosen by him to "bring praise to His glory" (verse 12).

So when you come up from your times of prayer, having repented of your sins, having received God's renewing and cleansing, you can walk into your day confident and forgiven.

You are his, and he is yours.

You are a child of the King.

$\mathcal{L}$et your father and mother have joy,
and let her who gave birth to you rejoice.
Proverbs 23:25

$\mathcal{E}$ven a sparrow finds a home,
and a swallow, a nest for herself where
she places her young—near Your altars,
Lord of Hosts, my King and my God.
How happy are those who reside in Your house,
who praise You continually.
Happy are the people whose strength is in You,
whose hearts are set on pilgrimage.
As they pass through the Valley of Baca,
they make it a source of springwater;
even the autumn rain
will cover it with blessings.
Psalm 84:3–6

$\mathcal{Y}$ou will eat there before the Lord your
God, and rejoice along with your household
over every undertaking of your hands in which
the Lord your God has blessed you.
Deuteronomy 12:7

I will praise You because
  I am unique in remarkable ways.
Your works are wonderful,
  and I know this very well.
My bones were not hidden from You
  when I was made in secret,
  when I was formed in the depths of the earth.
Your eyes saw me when I was formless;
  all my days were written
  in Your book and planned
  before a single one of them began.
God, how difficult Your thoughts are
  for me to comprehend;
  how vast their sum is!
If I counted them,
  they would outnumber the grains of sand;
  when I wake up, I am still with You.

Psalm 139:14–18

May the LORD add to your numbers,
  both yours and your children's.
May you be blessed by the LORD,
  the Maker of heaven and earth.
The heavens are the LORD's,
  but the earth He has given to the human race.
It is not the dead who praise the LORD,
  nor any of those descending
  into the silence of death.
But we will praise the LORD,
  both now and forever.

Psalm 115:14–18

May the LORD bless you and protect you;
  may the LORD make His face shine on you
  and be gracious to you;
  may the LORD show His face to you
  and give you peace.

Numbers 6:24–26

Happy are the people with such blessings.
Happy are the people whose God is the LORD.

Psalm 144:15

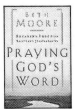
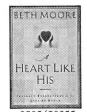
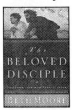